THE AUTHENTIC JOURNEY

Living an Authentic Life

The Authentic Journey

THE AUTHENTIC JOURNEY

Living an Authentic Life

The Authentic Journey

ONEDIA NICOLE GAGE, PH. D., CLC

Dedication

to all those who wish to understand those who are authentic

to those who are authentic

to those who are on the road to recovery

to those who saw this coming because you know me and like me anyway and remain my friend

SPECIAL THANKS

"You are the most authentic person that I know."

—Heath Butler, 2008

LIBRARY OF CONGRESS

Living an Authentic Life

All Rights Reserved © 2025

Onedia N. Gage, Ph. D., CLC

No part of this book may be reproduced or transmitted in
Any form or by any means, graphic, electronic, or mechanical,
Including photocopying, recording, taping, or by any
Information storage or retrieval system, without the
Permission in writing from the publisher.

Purple Ink, Inc. Press

For Information address:
Purple Ink, Inc.
1202 E 1ST ST, 14931
Humble, TX 77347
www.purpleink.net ♦ onediagage@purpleink.net

Onedia Gage Speaks

www.onediagage.com ♦ onediagage@onediagagespeaks.com

ISBN:

978-1-939119-85-8

Printed in the United States

Quotes

"I am going to keep showing you who I am until you see me for who I really am and until you believe that my representative and my authentic self are one and the same, and finally, until you believe that I actually exist so there's no reason to prick yourself or ask that question of 'where did you come from' again." Onedia N. Gage July 14, 2020.

"Too much energy is required to be fake. I'll forget what I did to get your attention if it was based on something other than authentic." Onedia N. Gage

"I don't do political well because I don't like being indebted to others. I never want what you do or have done for me to be thrown in my face or held over my head or blackmailed with." Onedia N. Gage

Other Books by
Onedia N. Gage, Ph. D., CLC

Are You Ready for 9th Grade . . . Again? A Family's Guide to Success
As We Grow Together Daily Devotional for Expectant Couples
As We Grow Together Prayer Journal for Expectant Couples
As We Grow Together Bible Study: Her Workbook
As We Grow Together Bible Study: His Workbook
Because I Do: A Working Marriage—Her Workbook
Because I Do: A Working Marriage—His Workbook
The Best 40 Days of My Life: A Journey of Spiritual Renewal
The Blue Print: Poetry for the Soul
From Fat to Fit in 90 Days: A Fitness Journal
From Two to One: The Notebook for the Christian Couple
Hannah's Voice: Powerful Lessons in Prayer
The Heart of a Woman: The Depth of Her Soul
Her Story The Legacy of Her Fight: The Bible Study
Her Story The Legacy of Her Fight: The Devotional
Her Story The Legacy of Her Fight: The Legacy Journal
Her Story The Legacy of Her Fight: Prayers and Journal
I Am.: 90 Days of Powerful Words: Affirmation and Advice for Girls
ily! A Mother-Daughter Relationship Workbook
In 90 Days: What Will You Do?
In Her Own Words: Notebook for the Christian Woman
In Purple Ink: Poetry for the Spirit
In Your Hands: A Dad's Impact on His Daughter's Self-Esteem
Intensive Couples Retreat: Her Workbook
Intensive Couples Retreat: His Workbook
Living A Whole Life: Sermons Which Prompt, Provoke, and Provide Life
Living An Authentic Life
Love Letters to God from a Teenage Girl
The Measure of a Woman: The Details of Her Soul
The Notebook: For Me, About Me, By Me
The Notebook for the Christian Teen
On the Same Team
On This Journey Daily Devotional for Young People
On This Journey Prayer Journal for Young People
On This Journey Prayer Journal for Young People, Vol. 2
One Day More Than We Deserve Prayer Journal for the Growing Christian
Promises, Promises: A Christian Novel
Queen in the Making: 30-Week Bible Study for Teen Girls

Queen in the Making: 30 Week Bible Study for Teen Girls Leader's Guide
The Secrets of My Success: Business Coaching How does she do it? Who does she think she is?
Serve the Staff: The Impact of a Healthy Social-Emotional Climate and Culture
She Spoke Volumes . . . And Then Some
Six Months of Solitude: The Sanctity of Singleness Notebook
Six Months of Solitude: The Sanctity of Singleness Prayers and Journal
There's a Queen Within: Her Journey to Building Self—Worth
Tools for These Times: Timely Sermons for Uncertain Times
The Vision Notebook
Walking Tall with a Broken Life
What Did You Say?: Affirmations. Encouragement. Motivation.
With a Crown and No Home
With An Anointed Voice: The Power of Prayer
A Woman Like Me: A Bible Study for Women to Survive Our Times
A Woman Like Me: A Daily Devotional for Women to Survive Our Times
A Woman Like Me (a sermonic study): Lessons for Us Women
Yielded and Submitted: A Woman's Journey for a Life Dedicated to God
Yielded and Submitted: A Woman's Journey for a Life Dedicated to God An Intimate Study
Yielded and Submitted: A Woman's Journey for a Life Dedicated to God Prayers and Journal

The Nehemiah Character Series

Nehemiah and His Basketball
Nehemiah and His Big Sister
Nehemiah and His Bike
Nehemiah and His Flag Football Team
Nehemiah and His Football
Nehemiah and His Golf Clubs
Nehemiah and Math
Nehemiah and the Bully
Nehemiah and the Busy Day
Nehemiah and the Class Field Trip
Nehemiah and the Substitute for the Substitute
Nehemiah Can Swim
Nehemiah Found the Mud
Nehemiah Reads to Mommy

Nehemiah Writes Just Like Mommy
Nehemiah, the Hot Dog, and the Broccoli
Nehemiah's Family Vacation
Nehemiah's Favorite Teacher Returns to School
Nehemiah's First Day of School
Nehemiah's Sister Moved
Nehemiah's Visit to the Hospital

Dear Authentic Seeker:

When my classmate stated that I was the most authentic person he knew, I was overwhelmed and excited, complimented and recharged, all at the same time. I exhaled slowly because that was the first time who I was had a title and a definition.

I was relieved that I finally could explain how my mind, my life's philosophy, and my words worked.

For many years, I was the person who everyone could count on to share the truth in a direct manner, sometimes altering their views of themselves, or other information that no one is ready for. I have made employees cry, boyfriends leave, and associates cringe. In various ways, I have shared my true feelings in a manner that often dismantled their dignity.

My supervisor advised me one day that I should consider changing my approach and my communication techniques. She was correct. Just because I was right does not mean that others are ready or equipped to receive it and especially with my direct delivery method.

It seems that I have a way, a look, and a demeanor that causes people to reconsider approaching me in some circumstances.

In this book, I will share some of my techniques and shortcomings, my philosophies and advice. I live differently. I love differently. I create opportunities differently. I pursue life differently.

Get ready for an extraordinary journey which will require you to reconsider almost every aspect of your life. Be prepared to be set free from the self-inflicted anchors, which you espouse.

See you on the other side of this authentic journey.

The Most Authentic One.

Onedia N. Gage, Ph. D., CLC

I want you to be authentic but not to intentionally hurt anyone.

TABLE OF CONTENTS

Dedication	7
An Authentic Address	17
Authentic Defined	25
What it is not	29
Who are you?	31
What do others think about you?	35
What is your story?	37
What does your life say about you?	43
How did you get here: fake, strategic, political?	47
My Story	55
Transition to Authentic	63
Discard your baggage	69
Acknowledge your feelings	73
Stop lying, planning, scheming, WIIFM	77
Being okay with being respected but not necessarily popular	85
Establish some rules, boundaries	87
Make new friends	95
Reconcile your issues	97
How will you transform from now to authentic	101
Start living it: How will you live an authentic life?	103

Conclusion: The Authentic Charge 105

Acknowledgments 109
About the Authentic One 111

living

an

authentic

life

Authentic Defined

authentic 🔊

[aw-**then**-tik]   ● Phonetic (Standard) ○ IPA

adjective

1. not false or copied; genuine; real:
   an authentic antique.
2. having an origin supported by unquestionable evidence; authenticated; verified:
   an authentic document of the Middle Ages;
   an authentic work of the old master.
3. representing one's true nature or beliefs; true to oneself or to the person identified:
   a story told in the authentic voice of a Midwestern farmer;
   a senator's speech that sounded authentic.
4. entitled to acceptance or belief because of agreement with known facts or experience; reliable; trustworthy:
   an authentic report on poverty in Africa.
5. *Law.* executed with all due formalities:
   an authentic deed.
6. *Music.*
   a. (of a church mode) having a range extending from the final to the octave above. Compare plagal.
   b. (of a cadence) consisting of a dominant harmony followed by a tonic.
7. *Obsolete.* authoritative.

Authentic is defined as not fake or copied, genuine, real, and one's true self and being true to oneself. If we consider those defining words, what of those words were a surprise? Hopefully, none of them.

'Not false' is the most complicated. In this world, we subscribe to so many societal norms, most of which are the opposite of authentic. As you approach this new level of authentic, being false has to be minimized then eliminated. Being fake has to be omitted. The opposite of false is true. You will question how can I be accepted and authentic. Sometimes, those do not co-exist. It is simply impossible for them to do so.

Copies of materials such as books or worksheets are common. Companies and schools make thousands of copies on a daily basis. Authentic requires uniqueness—the complete opposite of a copy. Copies are exact replicas. Being authentic is not a copy or resemblance of anything that is available to the world. The copy is the hardest to avoid and recognize. We are attracted to copies. They are hard to avoid and harder to resist.

Genuine is the most important, but the most difficult to grasp. Being genuine is at best IMPOSSIBLE. Genuine is defined as not counterfeit and free from hypocrisy. When you consider the word counterfeit, you may think of fake money, which is a federal felony. In this scenario, being genuine and not counterfeit means being the hardest thing that you will ever do—be something opposite of what other's expect of you or doing what they want you to do when you would rather do the exact opposite. Genuine behavior and attitude mean that you are committed to a lifestyle and a life which will defy the societal norms, and achieve what you are destined to achieve without concern of judgement or ridicule. Being free from hypocrisy is quite a task.

Hypocrisy is defined as saying or doing something that you would judge, condemn, or criticize someone else for while doing that same behavior yourself. If you judge someone for being a liar, but then you lie as well, then you are being hypocritical. If you are a liar then you cannot judge someone else for lying.

Real is what people claim to be but are not actually real, although they wish that they were. People speak truth and live in that truth. Sometimes real people are judging and often lack compassion, as well as they neglect the concept of support of others as they attempt to be authentic.

One's true self is a sight! When was the last time that you saw your true self? Have you ever seen your true self? What would others think of if they saw your true self? What would you do if you were being your true self and someone rejects that because you are different? Your true self is who you really are at your core. We have dressed up our true self because we don't believe that our true self is good enough. We feel that we must layer it with things that appeal to others so that we can be accepted. Your core self is dressed like you are in a snowstorm at the depth of winter. Your core self is wearing an undershirt, thermal underwear, a shirt, a sweater, a vest, a coat, a scarf, gloves, a hat, and snow goggles. The fact is that you are not in a snowstorm; you are living a life that you are uncomfortable with because your acceptance is based on the whims and the idiosyncrasies of others, because they are uncomfortable with themselves.

Being true to myself is the hardest part of being authentic. Being true to oneself requires knowing who that self is and being able to defy the noise and be true. You will be required to take a stand for yourself while ignoring the outside noise which roars with the intention of drowning out your own voice when you are having very important self-coaching talks which reminds you that being true to myself is worth the cost which you will endure. This is the loneliest proposition of them all. You will be unpopular. You will be avoided. You'll be ignored. You will be respected. You will be admired. You will be distanced. You will be stared at. You will feel different. You will be treated differently; even from how you were previously treated well by the same people. Being true to oneself means dernying others as needed, an action most people have never done.

Being true to myself is difficult to maintain because you have to make difficult choices on a regular basis in order to remain true, and by extension and definition, authentic.

Being authentic is not for the faint at heart. You will be challenged. You will be tested. You will be questioned. You will be criticized. You will be laughed at. You will be left out. You will be attacked. You will face opposition. You will be hated. You will be envied. You will be watched. You will be studied. You will be rejected. You will be mocked. You will be inspiring to those who desire the same authentic lifestyle. You would not be popular. You will confuse your audience. You will be authentic!

You are worth the commitment and perseverance required to be authentic. You will face extremes in your journey. You will get weary from time to time.

Being authentic is a full-time lifestyle adjustment, almost like transitioning from carnivore to vegan or something similar. It requires practice. Sometimes you will need to start over, so that you can reach the goal of achieving authenticity.

Authenticity appears like taking a stand for the underdog, choosing the road less traveled, and remembering the reason why you chose this path, while encouraging others to do the same.

What It Is Not!

Authenticity is not short-term or temporary. Authenticity requires courage. authentic is not negotiable and cannot be separated into parts or pieces. It is either all or nothing. Authentic requires your all–your total self. This is not a weekend or holiday position.

Authenticity does not get breaks and does not use brakes. Authentic is not popular, but rather powerful in achieving results. It is not easy or simple, normal or common. Authenticity is abnormal and eccentric. Authenticity is risky and limitless. Authenticity produces a change, so your old self will disappear.

Authenticity does not acquire friends or new friendships. Authenticity changes lives in a manner which requires you to stand apart from the rest. Authenticity is not common, so it does not subscribe to the regular order of life.

Authenticity deliberately separates your life from the previously used excuses. This separation will eliminate excuses and eradicate lazy work ethic. Authenticity does not make you a workaholic. Work life balance is still the best choice for authenticity. Authenticity cannot effectively exist without hydration, nourishment, and proper vitamins.

Authentic is not boastful or braggadocious, haughty or self-serving, judgy or into self-aggrandizement.

Being authentic is not about grandstanding and showing off for the audience. Being authentic is not an excuse to bring down others or to be rude or to be unkind. Being authentic keeps your focus focused.

Being authentic is hard work.

Who Are You?

What do you know most about yourself?

This is by far the hardest question that you will ever ponder as a person. The answer to this question shapes the life that you will lead, live, and reject. Who you are shapes what you do, what you become, and how you live.

Who are you? What do you like? What do you want from life? What do you think life will be like based on who you are? So, who are you?

When you consider the authentic answers to these questions, you will realize that you have many layers and that these answers are not simple and are not absolute, rather it is an evolving answer and direction based on growth and maturity.

Who are you? Based on emotional, mental, physical, and spiritual details, you will be surprised what you find out about yourself as you investigate who you are. Answering this question will cause you to discover aspects about yourself that you may have forgotten, or never knew, or needed to rediscover or to revitalize within yourself. I developed a set of over fifty questions which gives an idea of who you are. This list was not comprehensive, but it is an intense look into who you are by exploring important details which shape your direction in life and your life's philosophy.

Are you capable of being authentic? Is there anything which prevents you from being completely and consistently authentic? Your pursuit of authenticity will be shaped by this information.

Based on who you are, what is required for you to be authentic? Are you able to be authentic? Are you willing to be authentic? What will prevent you from being authentic? Can you overcome the obstacles and or fear of being authentic? Who we are affects what we are willing to experience and experiment with. This makes a huge difference when you are becoming authentic. Authenticity requires you to address your deficiencies in areas which you may not be comfortable exposing to others. Who you are needs to be fully explored because that is essential to your success as you strive for authenticity.

You should be truthful and honest, transparent and forthright in order to experience your authentic self. Are you able to do that? Do you trust yourself to be authentic? Do you have the wherewithal in order to be authentic? Will you regret being authentic or not being courageous enough to be authentic? When will your new authenticity be most challenging? Rewarding?

Who will benefit the most from you being authentic? Who will your authenticity intimidate? These two questions drive the decision to be consistent with your feedback for being authentic.

This boldness will overwhelm others and possibly you so you need to be prepared for the activity and the results it brings. Your authenticity often causes others to move more than before.

Desire to be authentic is almost more important than any other characteristic.

So when you consider who you are, please consider the characteristic, but not the usual important characteristics, which assist your ability to be successful while being authentic.

Being authentic requires different behavior. You have to abandon the usual methods and protocols in order to be considered authentic. Authenticity is a defining moment. Once there, you will never turn back.

Be true to yourself. It is a valuable experience. Being true to yourself is worthwhile because it frees you up to live without a cloud over your head.

It is easier to 'people-please.' Much less effort is required to please people and to fit in as opposed to being authentic. Courage is required to be independent in thoughts, words, and deeds. In order to take a stand for a differing view, bravery is necessary. This is a phenomenon for some people.

Most people care about what others think so much so that they are willing to alter their activities, thoughts, and words in order to please that group of people. This is not a recommended practice. You will lose sight of yourself the more you try and successfully change for others.

What do others think about you?

What do others know about you?

What do you do with that information?

The thoughts that others have about you is not influential, or at least it should not be. I mentioned that my friend stated that I was the most authentic person that he knew. That was a compliment. Most people who know me feel the same way.

Every thought may not be great, but the most important thing to remember is that you control what they think and what they say by doing what you do. There's power when you realize that you actually dictate the narrative that others say about you. Don't give your audience anything that you do not want repeated or to be ridiculed about.

What do you want them to think? Behave like you want them to think. If you want to be considered prompt, then be on time to all events. If you want to be considered compassionate, then you will offer your shoulder in other's time of need.

Consistency is the key as well. You will want to do what you do all of the time. You want to keep your word. You should always tell the truth. You may say it carefully but you will always need to share it. Lying reflects poorly on your character.

What does that mean for you when others have an opinion of you? You use that to ensure that the opinion of others impacts your reputation, which you want to protect but not at all costs.

Don't lie on others for your self-preservation or for any reason.

Be trustworthy by your audience, which again means keeping your word, keeping their confidences, and honoring your commitment.

Use what others think about you to influence your authenticity to remain authentic. Others will try to get you to abandon the authenticity you are committed to. You have to remain firm in your quest for the purest authentic person that you can be.

Use it to be great.

What is your story?

What part of it do you tell?

Why do you edit/truncate your story?

What does your life look like to yourself? What does it look like to others?

My children grew up in a bubble so when they went out into the world, they were rudely awakened. I, of course, got a few calls about this. However, I let them know that they would be fine. Some of that worldly knowledge was overrated. Based on this, I knew that I had parented them differently that I was parented. Our environments were different, almost to an extreme.

I grew up in a moderately poor environment, but I never let that be an issue for me. I am not sure that I knew that we were poor. The most important accomplishment was my education. I decided that education was my key to being wealthier. And my escape from my environment.

I had a goal sheet of things that I wanted to achieve which I have kept for many years. I review the list quarterly so that I keep on pace with my goals. I have achieved things that were not on my list. This book, for example, was not on my original list of what I thought I would achieve. Consider the path that you have chosen for yourself or will choose. What will you do to develop a story that you can be authentic about and be proud of.

Your story is formed by you and the activities that you choose to do. Your story is a culmination of who you are, what you do, and who you will become.

The Golden Rule here is make sure that you do not alter your story in a false way in order to appear to be someone who you are not. Your authentic story is who you truly are; not who you would rather be or who you dream of being.

There is an idiom, 'fake it until you make it.' The phrase is not a good statement–this results in a false sense of worth for yourself. This means that you have to pretend to be someone that you are not until you are prepared for the role you are in or working for. There is enough pretending in this world so why would we add to that?

Being authentic requires that you study your position, acquire a mentor, and practice your position or craft. How do you understand your position or craft? You will need to watch and learn so that you can handle your position appropriately.

What is your story? The story that shapes your life, your character, and your work ethic. This story will be a permanent part of your life. Some of the parts of the story may be sad and some parts of great. Your story is not something that you will be ashamed of, regardless of your situation.

Some of the most successful people have been homeless, are without advanced degrees, and do not have much in the way of material belongings. Your story is not necessarily unique. People are adopted, educated, non-educated, abandoned, hurt, abused, and other tragic situations. Those tragedies are often used to propel them forward into the success that they now experience.

This is an overcoming moment in order to use the events or circumstances which could have sunk you, but rather you are able to transition into a success. This is the ultimate goal for all persons. This is an essential part of your story.

The difference between your authenticity and the usual representative presentation is that you share that story authentically. Do you recall a time when you heard someone sharing their story and you leave with a crinkled forehead? This seems to be the instance when you realize that some essential details are missing. So much so that you discount, then dismiss the encounter. In order to be authentic, you need to share the whole story if your story was designed and developed to help others.

Previously when I heard people's abbreviated stories, I would ask them 'why did they leave out the main details.' They then look at me wondering how do I know that they have left out some very essential details which causes the celebration cues to fizzle. It is hard to celebrate for you when we do not understand that you have actually overcome something.

My life was designed to inspire others to achieve their goals. I would have designed my life to make millions of dollars, but it may not have been as inspiring. There are parts of my story I have based on the timing of the event and the occasion. Not all information is for all audiences, but more importantly I do share the elements which will help propel others forward.

Success is not just defined as money. It is also designed to help others to overcome their distress and lack of motivation, which could be depression. All of the details are essential.

Authenticity is dependent on your ability to be transparent and honest.

People want to trust the person they are listening to. The only way that trust is cultivated is to believe in them. Trust fosters belief. Trust is hard to come by. Your **story** is critical to building trust. Your story is **critical** to building trust. Your story is critical to building **trust**. Your story is critical for building trust for the communication that you are working toward.

Tell the whole story. Why not tell it? Tell the whole story. It will cleanse your palette. It will free you from fear and reservation, from shame and irreverence, to complete freedom, so that you can share without guilt or shame.

The only reason that people do not want to share their story is because they are embarrassed. You do not want others to know what you have done because of your status or reputation. You do not want others to judge you. All of this is totally understandable. However, consider the concept that you overcame that situation and your authentic story will give others the opportunity to do the same. What if your story saves someone some heartache or money? What if you saves someone's marriage or relationship? What if you save someone's life?

Your story is designed to help others. It is not for you alone. You need to be able to help someone else. You are a vessel to help others so sharing your story is the mechanism by which you do that. Your vulnerability lends itself so that others can do the same. Marianne Williamson states, "When we let our light shine then we unconsciously give others permission to do the same." If that is true, then why are so many of us trying to hide behind our failures? That is a reality check for most of us. Those failures are not the definition of us.

I was a school teacher and there was a student /parent/teacher conference where the grandmother of the student said that the student mimics my every move. I was amazed at that fact. I had no idea that she was watching me so closely. She mimics me because she admired and respected me. She spoke of me highly and followed me diligently. I had no idea that is how she felt or that she admired me in such a manner. Once I understood, I determined that I needed to assure that all students are watching me in the same manner. The fact is that it was true–students respected and watched me.

I share with them what is needed at the time of their situation.

Sometimes we edit or truncate our story. We leave off details that we deem damaging or unflattering. The test of authenticity is will you share your story regardless of the potential judgment that others may cast on you. I have a sense that judgement will never actually result. If your story helps them to survive their similar storm, then they are grateful for your confession and transparency. You are helping them to address and overcome their life's issues.

When we do this, not only are we authentic, we are also trusted as a resource and source.

Every detail is not for everybody, so some details are not relevant. That does not mean lie; instead, it means that you are sharing what is relevant. Also, you need to tell ALL of what is relevant. Your story is powerful–so much so that when you share it yourself, others respect you more and your past no longer brings you shame. When you tell your own story, others cannot use it to discredit or blackmail you.

When you are transparent, then others are empowered to do the same.

What does your life say about you?

What do you want your life to say about you?

The life I am referring to is your lifestyle–your career, home, car, social status, and other material details that some weigh so heavily when they decide how much, if at all, to respect, to like or to dismiss. Yes, it is true. People decide their relationship with others based on their material belongings and social status (old money versus new money versus no money). Money should not define your life, but material items, including money, will give a perspective on your life.

Humble beginnings mean being born in a relatively poor environment. The silver spoon means that you have been born into wealth. Those are the ends of the extremes. Your parent's and family's economic situation is not guaranteed to be yours, in either situation. Whether you will be wealthy or poor is related to your work ethic and you are in control of that work ethic and your career choice.

There is an assumption that a person will have the same financial status that their parents have/had. That is not necessarily true. That depends on work ethic.

You have an opportunity to change a legacy and you should change it for the positive. You will be judged by your outward appearance, the car you drive, your hair, and everything else that others can see.

You again control the narrative. I taught eighth grade math one year. In that class, I taught measurement, specifically surface area. This was the lowest performing category on the state standardized test. I shared with my class that because they know how and when to use the formula for surface area, that they had a chance to change the legacy of their family based on this newly acquired knowledge. Their families were defined as poor. This knowledge could change the trajectory of their families.

This means that what your life looks like can change with knowledge and diligence. This applies to everyone.

Being authentic means that you pursue your work and career in such a way that you understand your role in the success that you seek. It also means that you will pursue your dreams and goals without excuse.

You will have the opportunity to set a course of which you can be proud. Please feel free to make up your own mind and follow your own path. One day my daughter mentioned that she could not quit basketball because she needed it to go to college. I shared that was not true. I then went on to tell her that basketball was her choice, not mine. I added quite fiercely that if I was going to live vicariously through her then she would have been a gymnast or a swimmer. She was quite surprised at all of that information. She did not realize that her choice was her alone–that I had no influence on that choice. I had simply supported her activity.

Living an Authentic Life is about understanding who you are and not hiding it. Your childhood dreams and talents may have been suppressed because that career did not yield enough money. That may be true but you just put money over happiness and fulfillment. You will be essentially miserable. Authenticity requires the courage to do what you really love without regard for the financial constraints that may accompany that choice. This choice may also garner distance from those close to you, but at some point they will understand, reconnect, and get over it. Be courageous enough for that so that you do not live a regret-filled life.

Making lifestyle choices based on other's opinions and pressure is the opposite of authentic.

Your lifestyle is a reflection of your choices. Be ready to answer questions, but you should not have to defend your choices.

There is also the concern that you will be successful while your family may not be successful. This is an area where remorse for your success may happen. This happens from time to time. Your family and friends may attempt to make you feel guilty for overcoming those obstacles; that you have defied statistics. Please do not let that discourage you.

Your lifestyle can contain whatever you would like: any car, any home, any clothing, and any career. How will you achieve those goals? How will you acquire those material possessions? Map out your goals and work on your path. Do not let fear stand in your way.

What do you envision for the rest of your life? How will you live authentically as a result of that vision?

How did you get here: fake, strategic, political?

Forgotten what your real self looks and feels like, talks, and acts like?

Our lives have been wrapped up with image and the thoughts of others. We work hard at fitting in and being accepted and acceptable. Fake is defined as being someone that you are not. Not being authentic in order to make someone else comfortable is also being fake. Why do we participate in being fake? What is the benefit of being fake? Popularity? Being accepted?

Why are these people so important to impress? Do they care about you in the same manner? Do they try to impress you in the same way that you try to impress them? Probably not. There is a statement by Dave Ramsey, a financial guru, which says, "We buy things we don't need with money that we don't have to impress people that we don't like." This is the important message because we do not remember that it is not important to impress them.

Fake is an act. "The Oscar goes to . . ." But why is fake the mechanism by which we choose to live? What do you gain from that?

I hate opportunists. Opportunists are people who have a motive and they are scheming on how to achieve the goal, whether ethical or not. They go out of their way to figure out and do whatever it takes to achieve that goal by any means necessary, regardless of how it makes another person feel or if they hurt someone in the process. Opportunists are people who do not have any regard for others. They also subscribe to the 'what is in it for me' mentality. They only do what benefits them. Before they help anyone, if they ever do, they want to know how that benefits them. If it does not benefit them, then they do not participate.

They place importance on image and labels, brands and trends. They keep tabs on the worldly trends and status. They seek social and economic status. They seek popularity and leverage. They like bargaining power. They like being owed favors.

Political gurus are interesting because they are driven toward winning at whatever cost. They do not actually care about what happens to others. They do it at all costs. They risk it all for the political capital. Political gurus are researchers. They study the weaknesses and strengths of each opponent and adversary. They know each thing that motivates their opponent or potential opponent because they need to be able to bargain and negotiate the best outcome for them or their opponents.

Political prowess is a delicate and powerful skill. They spend time crafting their skills so that they can effect change. They do 'favors' so that people will owe them. They have blackmailing power over people for personal reasons and gains.

These fakes, opportunists, and political people may not be able to stop their practices. They have developed these 'skills' but they are not able to turn them off. It usually spills over into their personal lives. The outcome is not worth the process.

Typically, those people are not trusted by all people, so they function in groups where they are alike. They are drawn to each other, until they face conflict with each other. They usually also are not genuine in some of their interactions which continues to create the lack of trust.

Authenticity requires trust.

Have you forgotten your real self: look like, act like, and feel like? When did you get lost and abandon your real self? What happened to make you abandon your authentic self?

We were born with a personality and characteristics that made us the people that we are until there is a change. Reasons that we change: 1) We saw a need to change; 2) We were questioned by someone we want to like us; 3) We wanted to fit into a group of people that we find valuable; and finally, 4) We see that philosophy and behavior worth repeating.

What is required to change your behavior based on what another person does? In most scenarios, I need a very compelling reason in order to change my way of behaving or thinking.

Oftentimes, we are so interested in fitting in or pleasing others that we will neglect or sacrifice ourselves. When we change and sacrifice ourselves to maintain the status quo, we sacrifice our unique perspectives on the matter. When we do this, we transfer our power to someone else. This is the time when we lost our original self. You did not intentionally do it, but it still happened. Your original self was honest. Your new self lies with the intent to soften the message and to create a false sense of security for someone that you do not know or like. And certainly, do not fully understand why that is even important to that person.

Your real self is the person who is wailing in the background when you lie or bargain, concede or fold. Your real self is dying to be present. Your dilemma is how to be your real self without offending or holding others accountable. It is not rocket science, but does require bravery. Courage is required so that you can be yourself. Otherwise, you will yield to societal pressures to be someone that someone else will not be threatened by.

Honest. Open. Caring. Trustworthy. Loving. Truthful. Authentic. Rare indeed.

Your real, original self is unique and highly spirited. It yearns for a healthy area to communicate, collaborate, and commune so that results can be achieved. We are leaving a lot to chance when we do this.

We are all on assignment. When you do not do your part of the assignment then you are failing someone who needs and is depending on your authentic contributions.

People will also try to connect who you are with our success potential. That is also not true.

Who are you? Have you seen yourself lately? Do you know what you really like? What do you really want? When was the last time you made a decision without consulting with a team of people? When was the last time that you only considered your feelings? Only looked out for yourself? Spoke your heart and your mind?

Authenticity requires that some of those answers become yes, recently, and immediately. If not, then you are in need of some changes.

Make a decision to remember what you like and what you want. There's a movie named Runaway Bride, where the main character likes the eggs of her current fiancée. Her choice is challenged by the other main character. Initially, she was offended and denied his accusations. Eventually, she decided to taste all of the egg types so that she could decide which one she actually liked best. After she tasted them all, she decided on one. Once she decided, then she announced that she had made a decision. The most important part was that she was able to address her behavior and abandoned her previous practice of just agreeing with the fiancées, maybe because she believed that her agreement made her more appealing as a fiancé.

That is what people do every day–they compromise their own desires so that they can present as more appealing. That is not acceptable. That is not realistic. This is not sustainable. You cannot keep that up. That cannot be an ongoing position. Have you considered that the person that you are trying to appeal to has no idea that you are lying in order to be liked? Have you ever considered that they would like you as you are, regardless of who you are or what it is?

The bride was not more appealing because she liked the same eggs that he liked. He liked her as is; just like she was. There is another aspect that we should consider: people like this false person that you present to the world. When you are no longer able to maintain those false details, then you are not the person who people think you are and you will have to explain why that is the situation. Now, do you lose those relationships because you were not the person that you presented? Do they accept your real self? Do you accept your real self?

This is all unfortunate, but this happens everyday. People do this for many reasons–money, influence, perceived power, and low self-esteem to name a few.

Who are you? What do you like? What can you do to reclaim your original self? What was so important that you abandoned yourself? What have you gained by giving away your identity? Are you able to recognize the 'reward' was not worth the 'risk'? Were you actually more accepted as this person rather than yourself?

Can you abandon your representative and return to your real self? What will that require?

A return to authenticity means that you decide that you are ENOUGH. You don't have to be someone else in order to attract people to you– some of whom will not love you regardless of who you are.

What are your ideas, dreams, and dislikes? What do you need? What keeps you up at night? What makes you happy? What do you need to overcome? What do you like to eat? Where would you like to travel? What will you need to correct in order to correct your current public image? Answering these questions requires time to answer and process and become comfortable with so that you can actually live authentically. You did not change overnight. You cannot return to authentic overnight either.

What does your voice sound like? What does your authentic voice say? What power does it speak? What does your life bring to life for others?

This will be hard; harder than you would like but the work starts with an admission that you are not your authentic self that you deserve to be.

Are you ready to admit that you are not authentic but want to be?

Read and sign below:

The Pledge of Authenticity

I, _____, commit to authentic words, deeds, behavior, works, and attitude. I promise to live according to my philosophy and mission statement so that I will not abandon my individual purpose and productivity. I commit to addressing my needs and issues so that I do not revert to my disingenuous practices. I consider the feelings of others because authentic does not mean rude, disrespectful, or classless. Being myself does not discount the worth of others. I will not judge those who are not authentic. Authenticity is a gift so that I can live freely, without debt or consequence because I do not owe anyone anything for who I am or who I am not. I will be authentic and I will be held accountable if I am not. I have the courage to live out loud and authentically. I hope that my life will provide others the courage to do the same.

Signed: _____

Printed Name: _____

Date: _____

My Story

I have been accused of and attributed with many characteristics, including intimidation, directness, and lack of consideration. I have been asked to lead while learning to leave people with their dignity. I have been told that people cry when we talk. I know that there are people who do not talk to me because they are afraid of what I will say. Some of what I am known for are not as a result of direct interaction, but rather from the perception of others based on my interactions with others.

I have not had it as rough as some, but rougher than others. At six years old, I witnessed physical abuse of my mother. Later that year, she left my father and left me with him. He cried because he did not anticipate that outcome, but it was a justified consequence for his behavior. That was the beginning of my childhood adulthood. From that day until this, I developed a mechanism to live, cope, and survive this life. And now, to thrive in this life. Part of that mechanism included telling everyone that I encountered my true feelings and thoughts.

I did not label it as such at the time. Later in life, I realized that it had an effect on my direct communication, which was also interpreted as mean, rude, and insensitive speech, which was coupled with the intent to intimidate. I would not understand the impact of my approach until I was mentored by a leader who cared enough to mentor me through the storm that I became and am.

She suggested that when I speak to people in such a way that leaves them with dignity. My leadership was absolute and abrupt. Not many know how to approach and understand me and my approach about achieving the goal and the outcome. She was able to see beyond the unintentional harsh exterior to the compassionate, sensitive heart which develops leaders and seeks the best in others. Because of her and my commitment, I started to better affirm the leaders that I developed and mentored. In the midst of that revelation, I was also surviving my own situations, both great and gory.

I am committed to the success of my audience. As I serve others through my various careers, philanthropic activities, volunteer commitments, and spiritual engagements. I demonstrate my care and concern for others. I am serious about life and its responsibilities. I see the good, even the great, in people. I will not forget those who invest in me; nor those who love me.

I am significant in my life's work as well as in my quest for excellence for others as well.

Because of some very specific factors, I am this person. I want better for others than for myself. Others need me to help them develop their own leadership capacities. I do that for almost every person that I come into contact with.

I am authentic because I don't have the opportunity to be fake. I can't be fake or strategic, political or counterfeit. I can only seem to tell the truth about the matters at hand. I am known for my direct and truthful demeanor because I do not have any other influence.

I realized that I was authentic because a teacher told me that she wanted me to be great but she also wanted me to present myself in a manner which helped others to receive my message. This was a revolutionary moment for me because it explained so much about how people responded to me, especially my family. People have avoided me for years based on what I say and do while communicating. I realize that my direct conversations make people uncomfortable and they may be intimidated because of my message.

It was further reinforced when I was an assistant manager at a retail establishment. I was in a conference with an associate who shared with me that she was afraid to talk to me because she knew that she would cry because I was direct about everything. I am not mean, but I am not always palatable to everyone.

There is a way to become palatable and authentic. With some polish and work, I am more palatable so that I do not offend as many people when I show up and speak.

When I am told that I am intimidating, I do get upset because I consider intimidation a choice of the other person because they have not chosen to get to know me. I did not do anything to cause that intimidation. I am not someone who desires to lord over someone else or take someone else's power away.

I am sad sometimes about how people respond to me, but I also realize that I cannot control what another person does in response to what I do or don't do.

Authenticity requires honesty and transparency. Authenticity is rare. Most of us usually sacrifice some factors/details so that we will fit in and be accepted. Being authentic requires being alone on some occasions so that you can actually be authentic.

When you are authentic, you may not be popular and sometimes rejected, maybe even discouraging so it is hard to be authentic but worth it. I have always been just on the outside of the circle everywhere that I am. I have faced that fact as my eternal reality. This is not a popular position. On the other hand, I am trusted by all whose path I cross or do business with and am in relationship with.

I am committed to authenticity because I do not respect the fake and otherwise disingenuous. This is not a safe place and there is not any peace when you are not authentic. I brag about sleeping well at night and waking up with a clean conscience when I talk about my life and lifestyle.

In high school, I was not invited to join a social organization. I felt slighted initially. Then I was hurt. Until one afternoon when I realized that I did not fit in. I found out that they were having parties where they were engaging in drugs, specifically ecstasy. My demeanor and behavior did not allow me to be invited. I was not able to fit in at that level. I would never fit in to that group.

As a matter of fact, I was never offered any drug of any description. I never even smoked anything or any other type of drug. I even dated a drug dealer and still never tried any type of drug. He didn't offer me any, but he also did not do drugs either.

Authenticity costs fake friends. That is not a real cost. Real friends honor authenticity because they are authentic as well.

Authenticity challenges relationships, starting with my mother and family. They do not appreciate my authentic mantra. They do not want me to share authentically. They would rather lie and cover the truth. I have asked them about the mysteries and secrets of our family. They refuse to share the truth about our family history. They refuse to address the real issues so that we could heal and grow as a family. I have been ridiculed and distanced during this tenure as a family member. I have asked if I was adopted because of how they treat me. I am okay with the treatment because they do not intend to be honest, transparent, or authentic. We do not belong together. At least not until we can do better for each other as a family.

My real friends are few because of my authenticity, in both words and deeds. Those who understand me remain and grow to be my friends. Those who do not unusually don't last and disappear from my life because of their lack of trustworthiness and honesty and transparency. I do not associate with people who use me or others for their own personal gain. Friends are unequivocally loyal. When they are not loyal, then they are not friends. I am loyal to a fault. But once I am no longer loyal, there is not a chance to win me back. I also do not measure what you can tell me. I have had to say to people that I hoped were close to me that they did not meet my friend standard, so I had to let them go.

I also realized that the distance does not hurt when the friendship is not real. I felt foolish. I felt dumb. I did not regret my complete investment though. Who I am is authentic, regardless of the lack of reciprocity.

My career has been interesting. My success has been based on authenticity. My lack of progress has been based on authenticity. I am proud of my path, regardless of that the outcome has been. I know that my colleagues and counterparts trade portions of their souls and give away their bodies in order to gain status and position, power, bargaining chips, and notoriety, popularity and negotiability. I do not feel obligated to do something immoral in order to gain the position that I deserve or desire.

There are people who thrive on using their power to persuade people to be beholden to them so that they can get the promotion that they may or may not deserve and for which they may or may not be qualified. Why do you people do that? Why do others allow it? And still others succumb to the temptation because of the outcome?

How much more will you have to do in order to keep that position or move to the next position? That is way too much work. If I am qualified, then I need to be considered on my merits, not what I can do to get the position.

Again, how does this outcome happen? Why is this a perpetual situation?

Relationships between me and a man of interest to me are certainly an area of authenticity, which has cost me in almost every relationship that I have been engaged in. I am not skilled at strategy which draws another person into oneself on the basis of something fake, which will not be sustainable. I want to be in love, true love, where we can be true to each other, help one another, and grow old together. I don't want to question the motives of him and I don't want to give him reason to do the same.

Not many relationships can boast they have been able to manage to love where they started or grew to in an authentic capacity. People get into relationships and marry for so many other reasons other than love. I am the definition of love. I want love more than anything, anyone.

What is required to love someone regardless of the material belongings or the societal influence? What happens when we love authentically and we lose everything? What about the commitment? Loyalty? I want to be loved regardless of what I have or don't. I want to love regardless of what he has or does not have. Love does not translate into power. Power does not become love either. I do not decide on who to love based on what he has. There is a song by Justin Beiber which says, 'as long as you love me, we could be homeless, we could be broke.' Love is consistent and not contingent on belongings and other inconsequential details.

Authentic love is rare. So rare that people do not believe that it actually exists. I just want to love with all of my heart, my mind, my soul, and my spirit.

Love is the basis of all things great, awesome, and exciting. Your sharing of love demonstrates the transfer of energy from one person to the other. I want that energy transfer with someone special and purposed.

Relationships need to be protected from the outside influences which seek to undermine and diminish the sanctity of the commitment. My authentic approach and immersion into my relationship is mocked and teased because commitment is traditional and unpopular. The rarity of the approach is respected but seen as unrealistic. Because of this approach, the desire to continue will override the status quo. Imagine looking at your mate and being able to trust and believe the actions and words and motives of your mate. This is what most relationships do not possess.

Authenticity does not normally exist in relationships but I am determined to make it happen.

Peace is synonymous with authenticity. Peace is rare. I am peace and peaceful. Peace is chosen. Lack of peace is chosen for you, based on your choices. I contend that my peace rests on what I do and what I don't do. I can't do wrong to others but I want peace. This is a lesson that most will never know or experience. In the meantime, I work to remain peaceful. This means that peace is not bought. Peace is not transactional. Peace is experienced.

Transition to Authentic

From something to authentic?! We have defined and demonstrated authenticity. To be authentic, you make a decision to change all of the areas which are not authentic.

- Stop lying
- Stop doubting
- Stop procrastinating
- Stop the fakeness
- Stop the strategy
- Stop the plotting
- Stop the façade
- Stop the politicking
- Stop the WIIFM mentality
- Stop the games
- Stop the disingenuous behavior
- Stop using people
- Stop giving the minimum
- Stop behaving selfishly
- Start investing in others
- Start giving to others–FREELY
- Stop the mistrust

- Start with peace
- Lead with agreement
- Lead with integrity
- Lead with courage
- Lead with conviction
- Lead with fierceness
- Lead with compassion
- Show your heart
- Share your spirit
- Speak your truth
- Submit your soul
- Conquer your fears
- Revise your motives
- Remove the veil
- Discard the mask
- Receive the love of others
- Destroy your calculated moves
- Restore your faith
- Rescue your skepticism
- Create a safe space for yourself and others
- Share yourself
- Forgive
- Forget

- Consider an authentic mentor
- Explain your position without being condescending
- Consider the feelings of others
- Consider the thoughts of others

The transition to authenticity requires your attention and your action. Authenticity is available to everyone. It does not depend on social status or socio-economic status either. It is a decision to be genuine and truthful, transparent and selfless.

You will not be popular. Start today. The benefits are being trusted and trustworthiness. The benefits include details that we have yet to mention, but we will. Everything we need to be authentic naturally, we are not and we do not. Authenticity is not popular so it is not natural. The transition may be painful and taxing. It is grueling when you have to maintain that mask and façade, the representative and the status quo. That is not a comfortable place.

The benefit of authenticity outweighs the sacrifice. There will be ups and downs in that process.

What will be required to become authentic? What will you change in order to be authentic? How will your family and friends respond to your new mode of operation? How will you be received? How will you be viewed? How will you be treated? When will you share with others your reasons for the change(s)?

The transition to authenticity requires a decision. You decide that you no longer want to be fake or shallow, beholden or an opportunist. You need to decide that you no longer want that life or that reputation.

After a decision and some determination, there comes focus on the work that change brings. Focus is needed because you will be distracted or criticized, ridiculed or confused when you decide and determine to be authentic. This will not be easy; no easy task indeed. It is actually easier to be a fake, lying, cheating, and/or scheming person. Being authentic requires that you STOP being that person and doing those things. You can't do both: you will have to choose between the fake, compromised you and the true, authentic you.

You will need an accountability partner as well. Decisions don't make themselves. Determination does not exist on its own. Focus does not maintain itself. All of these require coaching and accountability. Your coach and accountability person will push you to your limits. You will need this person because you will want to turn back–everyday, all day, until you actually reach the authentic measures that you need to reach.

Decision.

Determination.

Focus.

Accountability.

Then there's practice.

Practice is making sure that you are actually able to be authentic. You will want to quit. You will need someone to talk to which will be able to help you to reach authenticity. Being able to be authentic will serve your time and energy; money and team synergy.

Practice leads to purpose, promise, and productivity. There is a purpose for authenticity. Authenticity creates a platform for truth, transparency, and community. Authenticity builds and breeds a level of culture. Culture stimulates excellence. If excellence dwells within, then, your work will reflect that excellence. Excellence contributes to creativity and completion. Authenticity prompts genuine effort as well as a sincere life where productivity and purpose must co-exist.

In this process of purpose with the promise of productivity, you will be pushed and pulled; prodded and punished. You became fake and unreliable because it was easy, popular, and widespread.

Authentic does not come with a mask or a disguise. In 2019, COVID-19 became a worldwide pandemic causing us to wear facemasks for nearly three years. In that thirty-four-month timeframe, we had to sort out the real news about our current state of affairs versus what was fake news about our current situation. We learned much about ourselves and each other. We were made to understand ourselves and the world at a different level.

The transition will not be smooth but it will be worth it. Your health will improve: blood pressure will decrease, your hair will stop shedding or falling out, and your stress will decrease.

Authenticity frees you up from those unrecognized burdens that others don't see but can definitely feel. Not easy but extremely worth it.

Discard Your Baggage
No need to unpack
Simply Throw the Bag Away

Authenticity requires that you reject your baggage. What is baggage actually? Baggage is your past. Baggage is your memory. Baggage is your issue because of your decisions. Baggage is your image and reputation. Baggage is your paranoia and discontent. Baggage is your overthinking tendencies and your panic button: which you press when you are having trouble making a decision. Baggage is the denial of the current state of your affairs; your perception of your reality. Your baggage is not unique to you. Your baggage hopes that you always require the approval of others and needs that false sense of worth. Baggage claims your self-esteem and self-worth such that it does not function at the proper level.

Baggage is not transferable. Nobody wants that mess. Baggage weighs too much to continue transporting. You cannot keep carrying that around. You should not want to.

Authenticity requires packing light. On Southwest Airlines, each piece of luggage has a limit of fifty (50) pounds. If your luggage weighs more than fifty pounds, then you have choices: 1) transfer you overage to another bag, 2) buy something to put the overage in, or, 3) pay the overage fee. These options are unpleasant at best. The lesson is to pack appropriately so that you don't have overweight bags.

When I travel, I have the tendency to overpack. I have options that I don't really need. As a result, I only use about half or two-thirds of what I pack. There would not be a problem if I did not shop on the excursion. I had to purchase luggage in order to get home from some trips. That is ridiculous.

But what is more ridiculous is carrying around baggage with no trip planned or baggage with clothes that are torn and no longer suitable for wear. This is the same as when you are carrying around your old ways and behaviors, your old issues and fears, your old/new lies and false image, your stale reputation and your stagnant life plan.

These elements are the contents of baggage which you need to discard. Dave Ramsey is a financial guru and is credited with a statement that needs to be used much more often: "we are buying things we don't need to impress people we don't like."

In this situation, you are ignoring and overlooking issues that need change and actually matter because you are only considering yourself. You won't tell or expose the truth of an environment or situation because you are afraid of the outcome of your career, social status, and reputation.

You would rather be accepted amongst a group of 'thieves' and 'imposters' rather than require people to be upstanding and upright, decent and proper for the good of ALL, not just for a few. Your behavior says that you do this.

There are students in schools who do not give the appropriate effort to learn and have failed the teacher's class but in order to avoid a high and true failure rate, the teacher passes the student with a 70. Everyone is happy. The person who suffered is the student. The world is not comprised of 70's. The world is composed of survivors and failures. Survivors are competitors. Failures are not. Failures decided against the concept of competition.

The fault is the parents and leaders. The teacher could have taken a bold step and said no. I will not pass students who do not earn a passing grade, but those teachers are on the target list for non-renewal of their teacher contracts. So, in order to keep their jobs, they pass lots of incompetent kids.

Discard the baggage. Being authentic requires you to take a stand for all regardless of your potential suffering.

The students who were 'gifted' the 70 are those who cannot count your change at the register, end up in jail, and generally do not have any employable skills, and probably cannot read. Because of our faulty culture, both parents and students are satisfied. They will never understand that they just choose to remain under the poverty line and are defined as 'less-than'. They did not achieve that alone. They had lots of help. They will also receive ridicule and shame, guilt and regret, pain and suffering. Although they have the power to change it, they don't possess the desire to do so. They are critical of others who do change it. The parable about crabs in a bucket comes to mind.

This works on both sides differently though. The saddest part is then failing students don't want help and the responsible parents do not want to help.

Authenticity requires a stop to that mentality and practices.

Throw all of it away.

Discard the baggage—it is of no use. There is nothing inside that baggage that is of use; nothing is reusable, nor of value.

Acknowledge Your Feelings

Authenticity may cause you to address your feelings in a different capacity. How do you feel about who you are? Are you respected? Are you revered? Are you sought after? Are you in touch with the important details of your life and the world? Are you considerate of others? Are you concerned about others? And their needs? Do you attract people or repel them? Why?

When did you lose yourself? You were authentic once; at least one time, at some point in your life. You are not sure how long ago that was but it did happen.

After I realized that I was brutally honest and that authenticity was my truest nature. I have no problem with honesty and candor. Other people do not use honesty and candor for any form of communication. There are people who consider me crass and maybe even unprofessional because of my bluntness and my directness. Unfortunately, I cannot stop being me. I cannot stop being frank and authentic. This 'behavior,' while rare, is the motivation for any continued truth that I live. I do not like to lie and I do not lie or fake well. I do not understand the value of lying, even though it may hurt someone's feelings.

The feelings of others matter to me. I am not truthful or authentic, direct and candid, in order to hurt people, but rather to help them embrace an unfaced truth, which they were not able to embrace solo.

I am sensitive to the feelings of myself and others. So often we camouflage feelings with the mask that we are 'free'. The reality is that we believe things which are not true. If I tell you that you need to correct a word because of poor grammar such as 'irregardless,' then you need to receive that information in the spirit it was given. If I know something and do not tell you, then I am not better to you than a stranger. In public, you will be ridiculed and criticized, but I could have saved you that embarrassment. Details like poor grammar causes people to judge you. As someone who cares, I should share that necessary information. Being authentic follows this behavior.

Check your feelings and align your behavior so that your behavior and thoughts, feelings and words match. This alignment produces a reputation of consistency. There is no way that you achieve that solid reputation while being inconsistent and 'wishy-washy' or flighty. You don't want to be the person who others feel that you can't be counted on; that you change on a whim, so much so that you cannot be counted on for any decision or position.

This is not authentic. That is not the place you desire, or do you? Decisive people are trustworthy. Indecisive people are not dependable and cause confusion: again, not authentic.

Your feelings influence your decisions. We want to make decisions which are best for everyone involved. Our feelings sometimes stall that process. We need to consider making a choice which is the best but may not favor you in all instances.

Keep your focus on the most important detail: making the best, most authentic decision. Consider a situation where someone makes a decision for you as a child, then later as an adult you realize that the best decision was not made for you. Further, you realize that the wrong decision cost you some important opportunities. In addition, you can't change the outcome or the circumstances.

A specific example is allowing, or rather, not allowing, eighth graders to enroll in Algebra 1. The enrollment numbers and the staffing for the school is done by the principal and the associate principal. These two people hold the future of 1,200 or more students in their hands. Daily, they make some decisions.

The requirements for the best engineering school in the United States is a 620 SAT score, and five years of high school math. If a student does not have an advocate who ensures that those requirements are met, even before the student makes a decision to become an engineer, then that student has the potential to miss an opportunity to achieve the success the student desires.

This is the story for tens of thousands of eighth graders in Texas. However, specifically 72 eighth graders were denied the opportunity to enroll into Algebra 1 without viable reasons. Data and evidence were presented to the decision-makers so that they could add these additional classes. They decided to only allow 32 students to enroll in Algebra 1. Several of the 72 were more academically qualified than the original 30, of which 3 dropped out. Those spots were wasted.

The next issue was that there was not an explanation given for why the data was being ignored. It was revealed that it was about personal feelings. Between the two decision makers, they had problems with the other parties involved. Personal feelings interfered with the education of 72 students of which the parents had no idea.

Imagine learning four years later that the student needs a fifth math class in order to qualify for a life-changing scholarship and college admittance. That time and opportunity of that eighth-grade season cannot be recovered and the damage has been done. The pitiful part is that their parents are not knowledgeable enough to have made sure that they had the opportunity. Further, they are not proactive enough to pursue retributions for this missed opportunity.

Feelings can destroy your life or that of others. I want you to be aware of how you feel and acknowledge those feelings but all of those feelings do not require action. Inaction could be a better solution in certain instances. Be authentic enough to use your feelings appropriately, share them authentically, and ignore them when necessary.

You also need to be strong enough to use your feelings to take a stand for those who need an advocate, without regard for your personal needs or costs. Part of being authentic is being able to help others even if it may cost us a promotion or a career.

Keep your feelings in their appropriate position.

Acknowledge your feelings does not equate to act on your feelings.

Authenticity does not mean intentionally hurting others. You can be authentic and grateful, offering them dignity in the process. Their feelings matter too. Be kind.

Stop Lying, Blaming, Scheming, WIIFM.
Start Telling the Truth.

Authentic is the antonym to lying. Authentic dismisses blame and owns each action and behavior. Authenticity does not scheme or strategize. Finally, authentic omits WIIFM: What's in it for me? WIIFM and authenticity cannot cohabitate.

It is easier said than done. That is true. This means that talking about something is easy. Doing it is much harder. Not lying is going to be hard. Lying is natural or easy because of practice and the need to cancel the truth.

Lying is a protective mechanism. When one lies, there is usually a reason to protect one or more parties. If you lie, then you are protecting yourself or the person that you are lying to or a third party.

Consider the last lie that you offered your mate. Why did you lie? What was the result of that lie? Did that cause another lie to be told? Why was it important to lie? Who did you protect: yourself, the other person, or a third party? Did you actually protect the intended party? Did you benefit from the lie? Did you do more damage than 'good'? Is there any 'good' from lying? What happens if/when you are caught in your lie(s)? How do you recover from those lie(s)?

Authenticity dismisses the lies. You cannot lie and be authentic. That is impossible. Most people cannot survive the truth but the lies are certain death. Lies change the dynamic of the relationship.

Lies also change how people view you. They lose respect. They omit you from events and projects. They look at you with a question each time you speak. There is a movie called 'Why Did I Get Married Too'. In this movie, when Marcus lies, he always says, 'Know what I'm saying.' So when he tells the truth, his friends are surprised. The next shocker was the news that he delivered.

You do not want this to be you. Don't be the person who never speaks the truth so people barely listen or you are the butt of all of the jokes. Liars are not respected and they are disrespected. Liars are not trusted. They cannot be trusted with information and secrets, not loyalty and integrity.

What do you share with liars? Not much. What does lying do to you personally? When do you decide not to lie anymore? Would getting caught in your lies stop you from lying? Maybe if someone gets hurt? What if you realize that the lies are reciprocal? Hopefully at some point, you will be able to live free and tell the truth.

You have dated people that you lied to and maybe that person lied to you. At what point, do you lose interest in that person and the relationship because of the lies, which then becomes distrust.

Don't be a person who is distrusted. Choose authentic. Life is better when you are free from lies. Your blood pressure would be lower. You would be less anxious. You would be able to look people in the eye with whom you are speaking. Truth frees up your memory. You will not have to remember the lies that you have told.

I wish that you will discover the courage to tell the truth 100% of the time to 100% of the people so that you can be 100% free. Peace awaits, your true peace, once you stop finding the reasons and the need to lie.

Being authentic means that you are an owner of your 'stuff' and life. If you were bold and brave enough to plan that behavior, then own it and accept all possible consequences.

When a husband cheats, and lies, why doesn't he just tell his wife? More importantly, if you are afraid to lose your wife, to lose half of your amassed material possessions, to experience limited time with your children, and to pay child support, then why did you plan to cheat and actively carry out that plan?

Authenticity requires you to address the issue(s) in your marriage. Do you think that she may want to meet your needs? Do you consider that she cares but does not know what to do? Further, how would you feel if she did what you have done or are doing? Communicates authentically. Yes, easier said than done. Consider what it's worth in order to reach a great place in your relationship. Remember that when you cheat, you are hurting two women, the number of children and the extended families. Cheating is selfish.

I can speak to those matters because I cheated after I felt neglected in my marriage. Rather than stay and try for the fiftieth time to mention it to him, three counselors later, and him talking on the phone to one of my bridesmaids, I walked away. I gave up a lot more than I should have and sacrificed more than was necessary, but I walked away because I could not see any other way. I am still paying for some of that but I am free.

Authenticity requires that I face that every day; sometimes several times each day. I don't regret leaving him. My kids and I are still healing. Owning it means that I feel free to share this with you—a complete stranger, a close friend, maybe even my future husband. Authentic means that I do not dwell on that past, I embrace my future, and I behave responsibly with my future.

Owning 'it' and being authentic also means that I don't blame someone else. Could I have adjusted my expectations, altered my needs, or anything so that I could overcome our issues? It is true that there are MANY marriages in which one person is holding it together with glue, glitter, and painters tape. I did not choose to do that after that second counselor.

Stop blaming others for whatever is or is not happening. One of the facts of life is that you are not trying hard enough. When you don't try hard enough, you don't know what you will receive and what you will miss. Blame is inappropriate. While others may have contributed to the situation, the fault and consequences will be yours. Blame is a cowardice response.

Blame is not authentic. Some things are harder to own than others. Recognize the consequences of your actions. Choose your behavior wisely. These behaviors can cost you: careers, family, criminal activities, and reputation. You cannot afford to fail in these areas because you will stall your life.

Stop blaming other people for what you have done. Stop doing things which cause you to need to blame others. Manage the company that you keep carefully so that you don't have to be part of issues which relate to tragic moments.

Schemes are defined as manipulation and deceit. Schemes are used when you don't have the talent or skills to achieve the same or better objectives. Schemes work in the short term but in the long term, they fail.

Recently, I encountered a person who changed the intent of the conversation and it ended with me explaining to her that I do not do business with deceitful people. Make your intentions known upfront–that's authentic. I did not respect her approach so I let her keep her money and her perceived influence, but in the end, I walked away because I do not bend to schemers. Those are people who you hate to see coming and can't wait to see them leave.

Schemers are also considered cheaters. Cheaters lack integrity. Integrity is important to authenticity, because it is how you gain trust and respect. When people do not trust you, then they do not respect you. What will you actually achieve without those elements? Not very much.

Authentic requires respect, and trust and the abandonment of the WIIFM. What's in it for me? Opportunists, non-authentic people do this! What am I going to get in order to help another person? This is not the authentic approach. If you first consider what you will receive before you do something for someone, then you may be considered selfish, an opportunist, and a self-focused person.

I want you to understand that you are what others see of you. If you want them to see something different then you need to show them something different.

Everyone wants to be compensated and rewarded. There is nothing wrong with that. My issue is that we lead with that when we should lead with compassion and care. Authenticity stimulates kindness for people as well.

WIIFM is not about others. Authenticity is also not all about you. Sharing your gifts and knowledge with others is not preventing you from being successful. You don't lose anything when you share with others.

People will see you as genuine and helpful which adds respect and resourcefulness.

TRUTH: start telling the truth. Stop lying.

Telling the truth is the crucial part of being authentic. Antonyms of authentic include fake, counterfeit, untrustworthy, and ungenuine.

Lies and liars are not authentic, which does not need any elaboration or explanation. Liars lie because they cannot confess to the truth. Their self-esteem does not allow them to be transparent. They have excuses about why they lie. They claim that they don't tell the truth because the truth will hurt. The response needs to be either stop lying or please stop talking to me. They may never stop lying. Liars are not able to stop that behavior and usually don't actually consider the feelings of or needs of others.

I hosted a talk show on internet radio in which I stated that if you decide to cheat then why don't you tell your mate beforehand. Why can't you just tell your mate that you need or want someone or something else? At least give them a choice. The problem is that they don't want them to have a choice, especially in that scenario. Imagine the freedom to let someone know that you are making a different choice and allowing the other party to do the same.

Would you agree that most narcissists are liars? While all liars are not narcissists, they are known as manipulators. Whether you agree or not and whether that statement is true or not is not the most important part of this discussion. The most important detail is that authentic people are not liars. And for that matter, narcissists are not authentic either. Solution? It is possible. In order to stop lying, there are a series of steps that one must take: 1) stop doing activities that may result in your needing or wanting to lie in order to save something that may not only be broken but irreparable; 2) write down the truth and practice saying it out loud; 3) practice addressing consequences so that when you are faced with those consequences you won't be so inclined to actually lie; 4) figure out how to be comfortable with the truth; however, painful it may be for you and others; and, 5) address your shortcomings and idiosyncrasies so that you will know what your actual truth is.

There is difficulty in truth. The hardest part is ending relationships, any of them. I cannot decide which is worse: the family or the personal relationships. You cannot seem to fathom ending that affair, marriage or roommate relationship because you are not comfortable enough with yourself in order to be alone, so you cling onto something familiar while searching for what is 'better.' This is not fair to any of you. If you can't tell one person about the other, you are lying, especially to yourself. Stop trying to convince yourself otherwise.

Truth. Is. Hard. To. Accomplish.

Narcissism is hard to cure. In order to remedy the narcissistic behavior, you make a decision to stop controlling every situation and everyone.

Authenticity builds rapport and builds community, rather than separation and silos.

Respected But Not Popular

Most people strive and desire to be well-known, famous and popular. This is important to some as a part of their identity. This is not necessary, but that is easy for me to say. I am popular and comfortable when people do not know me. I am not actually able to blend in or act incognito while in public. My family, especially my daughter, always asks if there is anyone that I do not know. I have to remind them that I am a native Houstonian, so I have been in the same city for most of my life. If I don't know people, then what was I doing? I have made friends, enemies, networked, worked, belonged to churches and other organizations.

In all of those interactions, I am respected, which is not always popular. Popularity can cause some people to lose their moral compass. Popularity requires fuel: it is similar to a car–you need to add fuel so that it can accelerate. Popularity has to be maintained. Others need to see you as popular and engaged in appealing activities so that you can remain popular.

Respect is maintained by being respectful, upright, and morally correct. Respect is based on your choices and decisions. Respect can be lost because of poor behavior and being inconsistent in all areas. Further, if your words and actions don't match, then you will not be respected.

There are people that you will respect. And those who won't. Don't throw your respect around. Respect is not braggadocious or haughty. Respect remains humble.

Popular is easy. Respect requires sacrifice and a discriminant disposition. Respect is not widely available. It is also unnatural, irregular and unique.

Imagine the teachers who were respected but were not necessarily popular, or not popular at all. What do they do differently? What do they do consistently? What do they do inspirationally? Why do they do it? What do they gain from their work and their contributions to others? It actually does not matter what they plan to do, what really matters is that they make others feel important and help others overcome their fears and issues. If others would follow that example, then we would be further along as a people.

Respect is not common. Shaping respect is also not easy. Respect over popularity. Respect over everything. Respect over anybody.

Strive to be respected. Start with self-respect then the respect of others is easier to gain.

Stop behaving disrespectfully and without regard for image and reputation.

Accept respect over popularity because respect will last longer than popularity will ever last.

Establish Some Rules
Establish Some Boundaries
Discard the Status Quo

Authentic personalities have rules and boundaries which abandon the status quo. Consider people who you admire because of their posture and position, speech and stance, level and leadership. Who are they? How did they achieve that status? How did they garner that respect? How did they gather that support? How did they establish that profile? How did they survive discarding the status quo? How did they decide to make this transition?

Most of us cannot be successful because we don't have any rules. Rules include a curfew, a bedtime, a time to get out of bed, and being on time to places. Rules also include who is in your circle as friends. Rules also cover distance between family members: can they borrow money, use your credit, live in your home, or benefit from your reputation. Establishing rules keeps you from failing yourself. Rules are not for them, rather for you. You need to learn to say NO. You do not know how to say no. If you know how to say No, then others will respect you, your time, and your resources better. There are people who you treat differently than others because of the outcomes which are possible based on your behavior, because of who they are and what they are known for.

Rules which are consistently followed and commitments are critical for the success as an authentic person. Rules help everyone govern themselves accordingly. Some people do not know how to follow rules or what rules even are. More importantly, why these rules are necessary.

Authenticity is based on your identity. People are usually disingenuous because they are trying to fit in. There is an adage that states: we spend money we don't have trying to impress people we don't like. It does not matter if I quoted it correctly because if you know it, then you may know where we are headed. Even if you have never heard it, you may still understand the concept. We buy things because of others. We remain in abusive relationships. We go places that make us uncomfortable. We keep jobs and pursue careers that we do not like. We suffer through: harassment, ridicule, and shame to be in the company of people who disrespect us. Reconsider the statement once more: we buy things that we cannot afford to impress people that we don't like. And we possibly don't like them either. It does not matter about liking the people or not. The problem is that you don't know yourself so it is easy to copy, and to mimic what you see.

Establishing rules then requires you to address yourself–your inner self– and behave accordingly. This person—YOU—will not be familiar initially but eventually you will. You will learn, grow comfortable with, and share your authentic new self with others. Because you are a unique person, your behavior, verbiage, and your mentality will also be a challenge to others. Rules are going to help you say no when appropriate so as not to overextend, say yes to things that are important because now you know what means the most to you, and share your feelings authentically, while leaving that person with some dignity.

Boundaries are designed to make sure that you maintain and, in some cases, establish some mental and emotional peace. When you consider your purpose in life, what you were put on this Earth to do, you need to embrace that purpose. Other people's negative influences cannot deter you from your contribution to this world.

Asking people to leave your space is one of the hardest acts of kindness you can do for yourself. You will have to excuse some people from your life because they are not aligned with you and some are absolutely against you. Friends sometimes fit into this category. You need to be well equipped in order to distance yourself from those who do not mean you any good. Every season in your life is not for every person in your life.

When you consider the disruptions in your life and the chaos in your life, first try to correct them with a conversation. There could be resolve in a conversation where you establish some rules and boundaries. People only do what is acceptable to them and they do it until corrected to do otherwise.

If that conversation does not help, then you will need to consider some distance. Moving people out of your life is difficult based on the level of proximity. Family is obviously harder than friends, while friends are harder than co-workers.

Moving people from your life is a purging process. It is not simple nor easy. It is necessary. We cannot grow and move into our next phase with the same people.

We all know a pacesetter. By Gage's definition, pacesetter is someone who is excelling beyond the coverage and with more aggressive than normal pace. My friends define me as such a person. If you are a pacesetter, then people will move out of your life because you are out of their league. If you are working some life changing events and your 'circle' is nervous, then that goal and project is the right one.

Projects and goals should be big and scary. The people that you share this information with should encourage and push you toward that goal. If there's any discouragement form those 'circle' members, then that may be a good time to move them out of your life, or at least your circle.

When your goals make others uncomfortable, then you need to reconsider that relationship. You cannot avoid your goals because of what someone else thinks or feels. That is called dimming your light so that someone else feels comfortable.

We are not going to stop living, dreaming, achieving, and building because someone else does not want to leave their comfort zone but also does not want to get left behind. Those two things cannot both be true. Ever.

When you start achieving your dreams, some people will leave because you will have less and less in common. It will not be easy. You may not be happy, but you will meet more people with similar lifestyles and goals, achievements and dreams.

Marianne Williamson wrote a statement which Nelson Mandela made famous. It reads: "Our deepest fear is not that we are inadequate. Our deepest fear is that we are powerful beyond measure. It is our light, not our darkness that most frightens us. We ask ourselves, 'Who am I to be brilliant, gorgeous, talented, fabulous?' Actually, who are you not to be? You are a child of God. Your playing small does not serve the world. There is nothing enlightened about shrinking so that other people won't feel insecure around you. We are all meant to shine, as children do. We were born to make manifest the glory of God that is within us. It's not just in some of us; it's in everyone. And as we let our own light shine, we unconsciously give other people permission to do the same. As we are liberated from our own fear, our presence automatically liberates others."

Once you understand your worth, which is connected to your purpose, then you will then understand that because of your purpose, you cannot walk around with a dim light. That is inauthentic. When you realize that others are watching you and depend on our work in order to make their next move, then you should be less inclined to procrastinate and avoid your calling and start with the consistent use of your gifts.

Imagine if the entrepreneurs who start companies which employ thousands or organizations which connect people had NOT done that. What would happen then? How long before someone will have to be given that vision to execute that vision, etc.? It is your role and purpose. It is your contribution to society and the economy.

Being authentic determines your daily work and the culmination of that work. When you are in touch with the authenticity then you will address your list and address the fears which accompany that list. Be ready to be great.

Abandoning the Status Quo

2.2 Kids.

4 Bedroom house.

Six-figure income.

Luxury car.

Married.

Retire from the same job after 30 years.

In 1990, that may have been the definition of success. In 2025, success is defined MUCH differently. Now, you are thinking that the author has two children, a four-bedroom home, a six-figure income, but she suggests the change of the definition? Yes, she does. I don't drive a foreign car and I have been divorced for well over a decade and no prospect for marriage. The new definition starts with are you being authentic about your desires.

My new definition for my success is multiple rental properties both residential and commercial, which yield over $500,00 each year, a paid off vehicle, several elaborate vacations each year, and doing what makes me happy, which includes helping and serving others.

Understand that the measurement will change as you achieve certain milestones, grow older, and address tragedy.

After 9/11, life changed for a billion people. During hurricanes and other weather catastrophes, people address life differently and material items are not as important as they once were. During and after the pandemic, I posted this on a major social media site: "It is a pandemic, something we never even imagined experiencing, so take the plastic off of the living room furniture, eat your dinner tonight on that special dinnerware that you received as a gift when you were married, and use those Bath and Body Works shower gels that you have been saving. Hundreds of thousands of people died without doing those things. Do not imitate them."

Events like that should change your life. You should be able to make immediate changes so that you can live and not just survive. That is all any of most of us have been doing: just surviving, and NOT living. And definitely not thriving.

Beyond the dishes, sofa, and bath gels, you also have not been on a trip because you are waiting on a companion(s). At least that was my story but I soon had to release myself from that thought process. You cannot wait to be validated by the presence of others. Authenticity does not live there.

Leave the norm and the usual for the adventure and personal growth which is affords. This is not a large ask or an unreasonable expectation. Again, living causes you to go further and expand your 'horizons,' leave your comfort zone and defy the odds.

The uncomfortability of all future activities and decisions will result in a surprising outcome. This is the goal. The history of your family, friends, and culture may be meager. Do not let those meager and humble beginnings and foundation keep you from dreaming and achieving what you set out to do.

This means that you will do more than your family members. Sometimes this will be difficult because you don't want them to say that 'you think that you are better than us.' Remind them that we all benefit with the success of any of us. Hopefully, you will start a trend and set off a chain reaction.

Remember to share with love, hope, and compassion. I taught a group of students who revealed to me that in their culture it was considered disrespectful to have a higher education than the eldest relative. This criteria stifles growth which limits your competitiveness in the world.

We have to embrace growth. We cannot hold each other back from their dreams and desires. It is not fair and it underserves them. Similarly, you will be underserved.

Dare to dream. Dare to live. Dare to change your legacy. Dare to elevate a generation.

The status quo should be abandoned if for no other reason than it no longer works. Be courageous. And bold. Even if and BECAUSE you are afraid. There is nothing wrong with fear as long as if does not stall you and your progress.

Make New Friends

Whew! In a previous chapter, we alluded to this. Now, the work begins. In the movie, *Jumping the Broom*, there is a scene where the groom reviews his friendship with a groomsman when he arrives at the conclusion that this is a tiring relationship and completely one-sided. The friend/cousin does not realize the nature of the relationship has changed. He also points out the disparity of their growth and achievements.

If one of you is growing and the other does not seem to be interested in growth, then the distance that is being established should be honored. Let them go.

Your overall progress will intimidate people in general. Your close friends should not be. If they are intimidated, then it is time to challenge them or release them. If you are similar to most people, then you share about 65% of your life, which includes details about dreams, desires, and next steps. Unlike me, where my accomplishments are a surprise or there was one announcement. If your friends are paying attention, they should be inspired by your growth. Hopefully, you are the type of person/friend that asks questions and listens to the responses. So you should be equally invested in each other's life.

Make new friends. Expand your network. Go to new events. Join a new organization. Start going to new restaurants. Join a workout group. Make new friends. Join a travel group. Reach out to former classmates. Make a wholehearted effort to meet new people. Your social media audience is also a place to cultivate friendships.

If you have children, the parents of their classmates and teammates are great prospects for new friends.

Stay present at events. Put your phone down.

New people will offer new perspectives, encourage you to continue your pursuits, and may also be a resource for what you would like to achieve. These new friends will provide mutually influenced inspiration because you will share your interests and find a common ground.

Find people with common interests–people who are already doing what you do or what you want to do.

Make time for your new relationships. The new friends that you should be authentic with and can hold you accountable for the aspects of your life which you may have avoided otherwise.

Everyone needs encouragement and inspiration but if you are the only one doing this in your friend circle, then new friends are the first solution.

FYI, don't confuse this with leaving those who are loving and loyal to you. I believe the new team is freeing. They are the people who ask why do you want that or isn't that enough. They encourage you toward your definition of greatness.

Reconcile Your Issues

We all have baggage. We all have a past. We have all needed forgiveness, and still do. We all have idiosyncrasies. We all have issues.

Issues are the things we bring into every room with us like a guest, but your issues are not productive, thus they are not welcome. Issues can stall your success.

One method of addressing your issues is to write it down. As you enter this level of authenticity, you will be okay with honesty, and transparency.

After you write them down, address a plan to resolve each one. Then, take action. Will it be hard? Yes. Will it be difficult? Possibly. Take a partner. Rehearse the conversations which need to be had. Make notes on an index card so that you remain focused on the important matters.

Resolving issues will include distancing from friends and some family. Part of the problem that you are having is that you have let them do and say things that you do not tolerate from the general public. You did that so that you could 'keep the peace' but you are not actually peaceful. You may have thought that it would only be a one-time incident. Now, 'that' behavior has continued and became the norm. This behavior threatens your comfortability and peace, your authentic nature and your attempt to keep a comfortable environment. So, it is time to address that behavior and the person.

People who are critical of you because of their own shortcomings and stalled life will also need to be corrected. That criticism weighs you down. It stalls your progress. It attacks your enthusiasm.

You will need your list to be addressed for maximum performance. You may think that these issues are not a problem for your achievement, however you have to admit that certain details weigh in the back of your mind and your life moves are based on that mental banter that you have. When you start to consider other people's feelings about your achievements and desires, then you are attached to an anchor that you need to disconnect.

Be okay with achieving more and have more education than your family and friends. Let's hope that they follow your lead by example behavior.

Be okay with not following the family business. If your father is a doctor, but you don't want to be a doctor, then be honest with yourself and your family. Otherwise, that is the start of the family tension. That is not wise.

Be willing to face yourself and your ideas. Accept yourself as is. Address what you do not like about yourself, then work on these areas. Get a coach or a counselor. There are professionals who can help with these matters. The authenticity which you desire can only be achieved when you transform from brushing your teeth in the dark to being able to turn on the lights to see yourself in the minor to being able to tolerate yourself to liking yourself to being confident about who you are.

Focus on yourself, affirming yourself and advocating for yourself. Forgive yourself. Give yourself a break. Reward yourself. Hold yourself accountable.

Keep the main thing the main thing–Do What Matters First.

Be okay with who you are. Correct the areas that you are not okay with.

The Transformation

How will you transform from now to authentic?

Transformation means to change. It is time for the change that you seek. The first step is to make the decision to change. The second step is to tell the most authentic person that you know. The second step is essential because of accountability. Accountability is the key to success.

The third step is to assess what we have discussed so far. What do you have the least problems with? What do you have the most problems with? What is the distance between you and authenticity?

This does not happen overnight, but it is a steady process which requires daily attention. This transformation will attract some unexpected attention. People will recognize the changes, no matter how subtle or gradual. The change may be discouraging occasionally, however you will need to stay the course.

You will need to remain focused and committed to the process.

The new idiom is 'Trust the process.' In this case, that is not good advice. If it was simple, then everyone would be authentic.

In this transformation, take each step we have discussed in the previous chapters. Start with the easiest steps first, which will be different for everyone.

There will be some difficult days. There are steps which you have already accomplished as you read through this book.

If you need help, then call your accountability mentor. If that person is not available, then call me.

You will be pleased with the results of the transformation.

Journal the experience as you reach these new areas.

This transformation will be significant and monumental—be present. Be intentional with your efforts so amazing will be the results.

Start Living It

How will you live an authentic life?

Today.

For the good of your life.

For the best of your life.

For the advancement of your life.

For the peace in your life.

For the advancement of your soul.

Start living an authentic life. This is the best part. It is similar to wearing clothes that fit after losing one hundred pounds. When you reveal the new body, everyone is amazed because they did not see the incremental steps leading to the big reveal.

The most difficult part is accepting the transition of the audience: your friends will change. Your family will change how they view you. Your professional colleagues will treat you differently—in a better way. Your social circle will honor the transition and your goals will be met.

Live humbly. Create a new life philosophy and life mantra. Remind yourself of what you wanted before you started pleasing other people for all of the wrong reasons.

Move the important items to the top. Accept your achievements and keep your focus on the future.

At times, people may say that you think that you are better than them. You may feel that way as well. However, that is not true. You have chosen to live and to do so authentically. At this point, you can only invite them to do the same.

Living authentically will set you free and elevate your peace and status. Authenticity is not popular, however externally respected.

Be confident in your newly respected roll.

Live it.

Live authentically.

Nothing stops you from being authentic except yourself. Dismiss the negative voices and the naysayers.

Live it.

Love it.

Authentic.

Authenticity.

Authentically.

Conclusion and Charge

Being authentic is not easy but it is easier than being fake or subject to someone else's approval. Authenticity affords you a freedom that you otherwise would not enjoy. It is not popular but certainly respected. This lifestyle is not for the faint at heart. It is not for followers or to those who need to consistently build consensus. It is for those who are ready to share their real selves with the world as they get to know who that real self is. We have so many distractions in this world. But we need to escape those distractions in order to become comfortable with ourselves. It may feel unnatural initially in order to be authentic, but afterwards you will be relieved.

Authenticity relieves you of stress and strain, ulcers and migraines. Your body will be more relaxed because you are not 'on stage' anymore.

Do you attempt to practice decorum and tact, diplomacy and compassion? Certainly. Do you still lie about why you are not eating the potato salad? No, you don't. Your answer is that it simply does not meet the needs of my taste buds. Simple. Tactful. Respectful. You are no longer putting the salad on your plate to make it look good, then wrapping it in a napkin and throwing it away. Just don't put it on your plate.

The Charge is to embrace your new ability to be authentic and free. This new posture will open doors while closing others. This is essential to living a whole life.

Be free to find your true and whole self again. Be true to yourself and those around you. Be careful to help others understand your new point of view. Keep your goals before you and work hard daily to insure that you achieve them regardless of the difficulty it may present.

Stay focused on what your inner self is saying.

Be authentic!

Live an authentic life! One that you are proud of and are proud to show your new attitude. One that others can trust and is encouraged by. One that inspires others to also be authentic.

The challenge is to remain authentic regardless of what is going on around you. Help others to reach their full authenticity.

See in the authentic zone.

Onedia Gage, Ph. D., CLC
07/13/2022

Acknowledgements

God, thank You for Your plans for me. Thank You for ***Living an Authentic Life,*** and choosing me to complete Your project. I just want to please You, God. Thank You for continuing to anoint me and to invest in me and my gifts, which keep surprising me. Thank You for loving and forgiving me.

Jordan and Nehemiah, thank you for supporting me and my endeavors. Thank you for loving me, especially when I do nothing without a pen and a clipboard, thank you for enduring my late nights, your ideas, the sounding board, the love and the support. Thank you for celebrating our legacy.

To my prayer partners and to my accountability partners, thank you for the long talks and the powerful prayers and the encouragement.

To the readers who this will reach and empower and touch and affect, may these words empower you and help you reach some resolve. May you be inspired to achieve your goals and dreams. May you enhance your relationship with God so that your other relationships will also improve. May you enhance your self-esteem through prayer and study. May you have courage and peace. Share love the best you can until you can share love without reservation.

nedia N. Gage seeks to share her outlandish pursuit of life with her love and work hic. She desires to share her advice with you in a manner that helps you do the same rough her example. She hopes that these words will motivate you.

lease feel free to contact me and share your progress.
nediagage@onedi...   , or @onediangage (twitter).
ww.onediagesp...

logtalkradio.com/onediagage

outube.com/onediagage

acebook.com/onediagage

Coach ♦ Advocate ♦ Teacher ♦ Facilitator
Conference Speaker ♦ Workshop Leader

To invite Dr. Gage to speak at your school, business, or organization,

Please contact us at: www.onedigagespeaks.com

@onediangage (twitter) ♦ onediagage@onediagagespeaks.com ♦ facebook.com/onediagage

youtube.com/onediagage ♦ blogtalkradio.com/onediagage ♦ ongage (Instagram)

LIVING AN AUTHENTIC LIFE

Publishing

Do you have a book you want to write, but do not know what to do?

Do you have a book you need to publish but do not know how to start?

Would publishing move your career forward?

Let us help

onediagage@purpleink.net ♦ www.purpleink.net

281.740.5143 ♦ 713.705.5530

www.ingramcontent.com/pod-product-compliance
Lightning Source LLC
Chambersburg PA
CBHW061802070526
44586CB00023B/2675